Francis Frith's
AROUND CHESTERFIELD

PHOTOGRAPHIC MEMORIES

Francis Frith's
AROUND CHESTERFIELD

◆

Clive Hardy

FRITH
BOOK CO

First published in the United Kingdom in 1999 by
Frith Book Company Ltd

Hardback Edition
ISBN 1-85937-071-3

Paperback Edition 2001
ISBN 1-85937-378-x

British Library Cataloguing in Publication Data

Francis Frith's Around Chesterfield
Clive Hardy

Frith Book Company Ltd
Frith's Barn, Teffont,
Salisbury, Wiltshire SP3 5QP
Tel: +44 (0) 1722 716 376
Email: info@francisfrith.co.uk
www.francisfrith.co.uk

Printed and bound in Great Britain

AS WITH ANY HISTORICAL DATABASE THE FRITH ARCHIVE IS CONSTANTLY BEING CORRECTED AND IMPROVED
AND THE PUBLISHERS WOULD WELCOME INFORMATION ON OMISSIONS OR INACCURACIES

CONTENTS

FRANCIS FRITH: *Victorian Pioneer*

FRANCIS FRITH, Victorian founder of the world-famous photographic archive, was a complex and multitudinous man. A devout Quaker and a highly successful Victorian businessman, he was both philosophic by nature and pioneering in outlook.

By 1855 Francis Frith had already established a wholesale grocery business in Liverpool, and sold it for the astonishing sum of £200,000, which is the equivalent today of over £15,000,000. Now a multi-millionaire, he was able to indulge his passion for travel. As a child he had pored over travel books written by early explorers, and his fancy and imagination had been stirred by family holidays to the sublime mountain regions of Wales and Scotland. 'What a land of spirit-stirring and enriching scenes and places!' he had written. He was to return to these scenes of grandeur in later years to 'recapture the thousands of vivid and tender memories', but with a different purpose. Now in his thirties, and captivated by the new science of photography, Frith set out on a series of pioneering journeys to the Nile regions that occupied him from 1856 until 1860.

INTRIGUE AND ADVENTURE

He took with him on his travels a specially-designed wicker carriage that acted as both dark-room and sleeping chamber. These far-flung journeys were packed with intrigue and adventure. In his life story, written when he was sixty-three, Frith tells of being held captive by bandits, and of fighting 'an awful midnight battle to the very point of surrender with a deadly pack of hungry, wild dogs'. Sporting flowing Arab costume, Frith arrived at Akaba by camel seventy years before Lawrence, where he encountered 'desert princes and rival sheikhs, blazing with jewel-hilted swords'.

During these extraordinary adventures he was assiduously exploring the desert regions bordering the Nile and patiently recording the antiquities and peoples with his camera. He was the first photographer to venture beyond the sixth cataract. Africa was still the mysterious 'Dark Continent', and Stanley and Livingstone's historic meeting was a decade into the future. The conditions for picture taking confound belief. He laboured for hours in his wicker dark-room in the sweltering heat of the desert, while the volatile chemicals fizzed dangerously in their trays. Often he was forced to work in remote tombs and caves where conditions were cooler. Back in London he exhibited his photographs and was 'rapturously cheered' by members of the Royal Society. His reputation as a photographer was made overnight. An eminent modern historian has likened their impact on the population of the time to that on our own generation of the first photographs taken on the surface of the moon.

VENTURE OF A LIFE-TIME

Characteristically, Frith quickly spotted the opportunity to create a new business as a specialist publisher of photographs. He lived in an era of immense and sometimes violent change. For the poor in the early part of Victoria's reign work was a drudge and the hours long, and people had precious little free time to enjoy themselves.

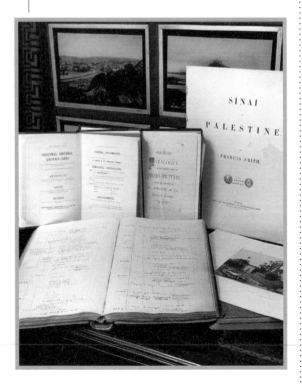

Most had no transport other than a cart or gig at their disposal, and had not travelled far beyond the boundaries of their own town or village. However, by the 1870s, the railways had threaded their way across the country, and Bank Holidays and half-day Saturdays had been made obligatory by Act of Parliament. All of a sudden the ordinary working man and his family were able to enjoy days out and see a little more of the world.

With characteristic business acumen, Francis Frith foresaw that these new tourists would enjoy having souvenirs to commemorate their days out. In 1860 he married Mary Ann Rosling and set out with the intention of photographing every city, town and village in Britain. For the next thirty years he travelled the country by train and by pony and trap, producing fine photographs of seaside resorts and beauty spots that were keenly bought by millions of Victorians. These prints were painstakingly pasted into family albums and pored over during the dark nights of winter, rekindling precious memories of summer excursions.

THE RISE OF FRITH & CO

Frith's studio was soon supplying retail shops all over the country. To meet the demand he gathered about him a small team of photographers, and published the work of independent artist-photographers of the calibre of Roger Fenton and Francis Bedford. In order to gain some understanding of the scale of Frith's business one only has to look at the catalogue issued by Frith & Co in 1886: it runs to some 670

pages, listing not only many thousands of views of the British Isles but also many photographs of most European countries, and China, Japan, the USA and Canada – note the sample page shown above from the hand-written *Frith & Co* ledgers detailing pictures taken. By 1890 Frith had created the greatest specialist photographic publishing company in the world, with over 2,000 outlets – more than the combined number that Boots and WH Smith have today! The picture on the right shows the *Frith & Co* display board at Ingleton in the Yorkshire Dales. Beautifully constructed with mahogany frame and gilt inserts, it could display up to a dozen local scenes.

POSTCARD BONANZA

◆◆

The ever-popular holiday postcard we know today took many years to develop. In 1870 the Post Office issued the first plain cards, with a pre-printed stamp on one face. In 1894 they allowed other publishers' cards to be sent through the mail with an attached adhesive halfpenny stamp. Demand grew rapidly, and in 1895 a new size of postcard was permitted called the court card, but there was little room for illustration. In 1899, a year after Frith's death, a new card measuring 5.5 x 3.5 inches became the standard format, but it was not until 1902 that the divided back came into being, with address and message on one face and a full-size illustration on the other. *Frith & Co* were in the vanguard of postcard development, and Frith's sons Eustace and Cyril continued their father's monumental task, expanding the number of views offered to the public and recording more and more places in Britain, as the coasts and countryside were opened up to mass travel.

Francis Frith died in 1898 at his villa in Cannes, his great project still growing. The archive he created continued in business for another seventy years. By 1970 it contained over a third of a million pictures of 7,000 cities, towns and villages. The massive photographic record Frith has left to us stands as a living monument to a special and very remarkable man.

Frith's Archive: *A Unique Legacy*

FRANCIS FRITH'S legacy to us today is of immense significance and value, for the magnificent archive of evocative photographs he created provides a unique record of change in 7,000 cities, towns and villages throughout Britain over a century and more. Frith and his fellow studio photographers revisited locations many times down the years to update their views, compiling for us an enthralling and colourful pageant of British life and character.

We tend to think of Frith's sepia views of Britain as nostalgic, for most of us use them to conjure up memories of places in our own lives with which we have family associations. It often makes us forget that to Francis Frith they were records of daily life as it was actually being lived in the cities, towns and villages of his day. The Victorian age was one of great and often bewildering change for ordinary people, and though the pictures evoke an impression of slower times, life was as busy and hectic as it is today.

We are fortunate that Frith was a photographer of the people, dedicated to recording the minutiae of everyday life. For it is this sheer wealth of visual data, the painstaking chronicle of changes in dress, transport, street layouts, buildings, housing, engineering and landscape that captivates us so much today. His remarkable images offer us a powerful link with the past and with the lives of our ancestors.

TODAY'S TECHNOLOGY

Computers have now made it possible for Frith's many thousands of images to be accessed almost instantly. In the Frith archive today, each photograph is carefully 'digitised' then stored on a CD Rom. Frith archivists can locate a single photograph amongst thousands within seconds. Views can be catalogued and sorted under a variety of categories of place and content to the immediate benefit of researchers. Inexpensive reference prints can be created for them at the touch of a mouse button, and a wide range of books and other printed materials assembled and published for a wider, more general readership - in the next twelve months over a hundred Frith local history titles will be published! The

See Frith at www. francisfrith.co.uk

day-to-day workings of the archive are very different from how they were in Francis Frith's time: imagine the herculean task of sorting through eleven tons of glass negatives as Frith had to do to locate a particular sequence of pictures! Yet the archive still prides itself on maintaining the same high standards of excellence laid down by Francis Frith, including the painstaking cataloguing and indexing of every view.

It is curious to reflect on how the internet now allows researchers in America and elsewhere greater instant access to the archive than Frith himself ever enjoyed. Many thousands of individual views can be called up on screen within seconds on one of the Frith internet sites, enabling people living continents away to revisit the streets of their ancestral home town, or view places in Britain where they have enjoyed holidays. Many overseas researchers welcome the chance to view special theme selections, such as transport, sports, costume and ancient monuments.

We are certain that Francis Frith would have heartily approved of these modern developments, for he himself was always working at the very limits of Victorian photographic technology.

THE VALUE OF THE ARCHIVE TODAY

Because of the benefits brought by the computer, Frith's images are increasingly studied by social historians, by researchers into genealogy and ancestory, by architects, town planners, and by teachers and schoolchildren involved in local history projects. In addition, the archive offers every one of us a unique opportunity to examine the places where we and our families have lived and worked down the years. Immensely successful in Frith's own era, the archive is now, a century and more on, entering a new phase of popularity.

THE PAST IN TUNE WITH THE FUTURE

Historians consider the Francis Frith Collection to be of prime national importance. It is the only archive of its kind remaining in private ownership and has been valued at a million pounds. However, this figure is now rapidly increasing as digital technology enables more and more people around the world to enjoy its benefits.

Francis Frith's archive is now housed in an historic timber barn in the beautiful village of Teffont in Wiltshire. Its founder would not recognize the archive office as it is today. In place of the many thousands of dusty boxes containing glass plate negatives and an all-pervading odour of photographic chemicals, there are now ranks of computer screens. He would be amazed to watch his images travelling round the world at unimaginable speeds through network and internet lines.

The archive's future is both bright and exciting. Francis Frith, with his unshakeable belief in making photographs available to the greatest number of people, would undoubtedly approve of what is being done today with his lifetime's work. His photographs, depicting our shared past, are now bringing pleasure and enlightenment to millions around the world a century and more after his death.

CHESTERFIELD – *An Introduction*

THE SECOND largest town in Derbyshire, Chesterfield's history goes back to the Roman occupation when a fort was established here, one of a chain of military installations, on the road between Derby and York. Until around AD 47 the line of the Fosse Way marked the temporary northern frontier of the province, but by around AD 70 there had been a gradual occupation of the area between the rivers Trent and Don. There were a number of small forts strung out along the roads of Cheshire and Derbyshire, securing lines of communication for the legionary bases at Chester and York, policing the local natives, and regulating the movement of salt and copper ore from Cheshire and lead from the Derbyshire mines.

It is hard to say how long the Chesterfield fort lasted. The fort at Derby was garrisoned until at least AD 350, and it is possible that it was refortified by the Danes around AD 913 when Edward the Elder of Wessex and his sister Aethelflaed of Mercia launched their joint offensive against the Danelaw. When Derby fell, albeit briefly, to Aethelflaed's troops in AD 917, the Anglo-Saxon Chronicle mentions that four of her thegns were killed within the gates of the town. It has been suggested that this refers to the Danes' use of the old Roman fort at Little Chester (Chester Green to those of you who know present-day Derby), but this is also a possible mis-interpretation, as the old Danish word for street is gata, and the fighting could therefore have taken place within the Danish civilian settlement which is thought to have been located elsewhere.

By the time the Domesday Book was being compiled, Chesterfield was one of six hamlets within the royal manor of Newbold, the others being Whittington, Brimington, Tapton, Boythorpe and Eckington. The chapel at Newbold was almost certainly the mother church for Chesterfield. Associated with Chesterfield is the wapentake of Scarsdale. A wapentake is an echo from the time when Derbyshire was a part of the Danelaw, and when Danish laws and customs, not English ones, were observed. Wapentake literally means 'show of weapons'; the Danish way of voting at public meetings was by holding a sword or spear aloft - a bit more colourful than simply having a show of hands!

The first written reference to Chesterfield, Cestrefeud, dates back to AD 955. Long before 1200 it had outstripped Newbold to become the major market town of north-east Derbyshire. The original market appears to have been located near the parish church, but in 1199 a new market was laid out on the western edge of the town. An indication of Chesterfield's growing importance is the fact that both market sites appear to have operated side-by-side well into the 13th century, by which time leather working, tanning and the manufacture of woollen cloth were all established in the town.

In 1204 King John granted the manor of Chesterfield and the wapentake of Scarsdale to William de Briwere. On Briwere's death his estates were divided between his children, the manor together with estates at Brimington and Whittington passing to his daughter Isobel. When Isobel married her lands automatically became the property of her husband Baldwin de Wake.

In the 13th century one of the greatest fortresses in England was situated at Duffield in Derbyshire and belonged to Robert de Ferrers, Earl of Derby. In 1263 the Earl rebelled against the king's authority, but was defeated by Henry III. Though his possessions were ordered forfeit to the Crown, the Earl was pardoned on condition that if he rebelled again he would be disinherited. In 1266, following the defeat of the barons at Evesham, Robert took to the field again. He assembled a force at Duffield, where he was joined by Baldwin de Wake, Lord of Chesterfield. On their way north to meet up with reinforcements from Yorkshire, the rebels were attacked by royal troops and forced to shelter behind the defences at Chesterfield. Prince Henry threatened to utterly destroy the town if Ferrers refused to surrender. The Earl, who was suffering with gout, hid in the parish church behind some sacks of wool left by traders at the Whitsuntide fair (at this time it was quite normal for churches to double up as warehouses). Ferrers was betrayed, captured and taken to Windsor in irons. The Ferrers estates were confiscated and Duffield Castle demolished.

When Baldwin de Wake died, his lands comprised no less than 148 manors. Eventually the manor of Chesterfield and the wapentake of Scarsdale were inherited by Richard, Duke of Gloucester, who gave them to Edward IV in exchange for lands in Yorkshire, including the town and castle of Scarborough.

Around 1278 Chesterfield merchants were able to grab a larger share of the lucrative market in lead at Derby's expense, thanks to the monks of Dale Abbey, who obstructed the navigable Derwent with weirs at Borrowash. Chesterfield was able to offer an alternative route to London and the Continent via the port of Bawtry on the River Idle. It is possible that the Derbyshire lead mining industry of the late middle ages was operated on some

sort of cartel basis. Many smelters and investors in mines were also merchants; in the 14th century the smelter Thurstan de Boure of Tideswell amassed a fortune operating bole hills and trading in lead at Chesterfield and Derby.

A bole hill was in effect a wind assisted smelter. It was a walled enclosure a few feet in

tion of iron-working, it was not until 1851 that Chesterfield's population topped 7000.

Breaking out in June 1348 and lasting until 1351, the Black Death swept through England and Scotland, leaving in its wake a decimated population. Recovery was hampered by further outbreaks in 1361-62, 1369 and 1375, pushing total fatalities to between one half

diameter, with an opening facing the prevailing wind. It was filled with layers of timber or peat and then lead ore. This was covered with more timber, then another layer of ore, and so on until it was full, at which point it was topped off with turf. A channel ran from inside the bole to a gathering pool into which the molten lead would trickle. When the wind was in the right direction the bole was fired, and the smelted ore collected in the gathering pool formed a 'pig' of lead.

Even so, Chesterfield would remain a small market town. Around the 1550s the population is thought to have been over 1000, similar to that of Wirksworth, but only half that of Derby. Even with the opening of a number of small collieries and the introduc-

and two-thirds of the entire population. The effects would be felt for at least two centuries. Throughout the East Midlands over four hundred villages were abandoned as a result of the Black Death and subsequent changes of settlement. The populations of Chesterfield and Derby may have held up reasonably well, their importance as textile centres and their involvement in lead mining probably attracting an influx of survivors from the decimated villages. Even so, the output of lead for the county as a whole fell to about half of what it had been in the 13th century, and in places like Ashford production ceased altogether. However, Chesterfield Fair continued to be one of the most important markets for the buying and selling of lead.

In 1586-87 plague once again ravaged the East Midlands. The execution of Mary, Queen of Scots inexorably led to war with Spain, but the plague was such that when Derbyshire held its muster of troops in November 1587, the men of Scarsdale were not present. The outbreak lasted until the winter of 1587, and its short-term effect on Chesterfield was devastating. Average deaths in the town before the plague were only three a month; during it they were 54 in June 1587 and 52 in July. There were two further outbreaks in the town between 1587 and 1609, and Nottinghamshire was ravaged to such an extent in 1605 that restrictions on travel were imposed.

As well as outbreaks of plague, another communicable disease was well known to the medieval inhabitants of the town - leprosy. The disease was known in England before the First Crusade (1096-99); by around 1150, Chesterfield, like all other boroughs, had a hospital for lepers. St. Leonard's was situated at Spital near the Rother, about half a mile to the south-east of the town. Lepers were required to wear something akin to a monk's habit. They carried a cup for the collection of alms and a clapper to warn others that they were near. The local and powerful Guild of St Mary, founded in 1218, had among its rules: 'If a brother, through age, or loss of limb, or leprosy, comes to so great want that he cannot support himself, the brethren who are able shall in turn supply him with needful food, or shall find for him a house of religion where he may stay during life'.

One interesting fact is that Chesterfield never experienced an outbreak of cholera. This particular disease was prevalent throughout England in the mid-19th century, and was associated with inadequate sewage disposal and contaminated water supplies.

THE AGE OF INDUSTRIALISATION

Chesterfield's early industries included leather working, and among the town's products were leather 'jacks', large liquor jugs made from waxed leather and coated on the outside with tar. In the 10th century leather workers often carried out all the processes themselves, stripping the skin, curing, stretching and dyeing. Their workshops would have smelled very unpleasant, as dung was used in some processes and urine in others. Tanning became an industry in its own right; more than one local medieval will refers to things like the 'netting toobe', 'sorry dog skins', 'white leather' and so on. 'Netting' is an old Derbyshire word for urine and the 'toobe' was the tub where tanners used to store it. 'White leather' was horse skin cured with lime. This type of skin was quite tough, and found a number of uses including laces and parchment. 'Sorry dog skins', on the other hand, were poor quality skins, including dog, as in medieval England the word sorry also meant 'of little value'. We have already mentioned the town's strong links with the lead mining industry, but there was also nail making, and from the mid-16th century a number of small collieries operated in the locality.

With locally available supplies of iron ore, coal, and water, the earls of Shrewsbury were active in promoting iron-making. A blast furnace was active at Stretton in 1593, and by 1606 a furnace and forge had opened at Barlow. By the mid-17th century there were five blast furnaces at work in the vicinity, but due to competition from cheap imports from Sweden this fell. By 1740 there were only four blast furnaces at work in the whole county.

Local iron-making received a boost in the 1770s when John Smith took over a furnace, foundry, forge and boring mill at Brampton with the intention of getting into the growing market for castings, especially for steam engines. The Smiths came from Sheffield, where the family had been involved in the cutlery trade since at least the early 17th century. The original partners for this new venture were John Smith, Samuel Allsop and John Ernest Sanor. The Brampton site was renamed the Griffin Works; in the early years it was pretty well self contained, in that there were local supplies of dog-toothed iron-ore, coal, and water. The outbreak of the American War of Independence saw the Griffin Works switch more and more to the production of armaments, especially cannon. This led Smith to open the Adelphi Works as a munitions plant, manufacturing cannon

balls and shells for the army and the East India Company. The iron industry would be further boosted by the opening of the Chesterfield Canal in 1777, of which the Adelphi had its own branch. The Smiths enhanced the quality of Derbyshire iron founding by introducing coke-fired blast furnaces into the county. At its height the Smith empire employed 1200 workers at various sites including Calow Iron Works, Calow, and the Newcross Foundry, Swann Street, Manchester.

The Smiths journey books for the years 1824 to 1835 still exist. They are a fascinating insight into the world of business during the early decades of the 19th century. The board members would take it in turns to go off on sales and debt collecting trips around the country. In 1824 Joseph Bright Smith took a trip down to the south of England with calls at Birmingham, Bristol and Brighton. His journey took 61 days; the stagecoach to London took about sixteen hours, and to Birmingham

around seven hours. Joseph came back with £3905, his expenses having amounted to only £53 17s 0d.

The coming of the railways in the 1830s was a further boost to local industries. The Clay Cross Co were the first to send coal to London by rail, and in 1846 the Earl of Stanhope granted Benjamin and Josiah Smith a lease for ironstone, coal and fireclay in the parishes of Dale and Stanton-by-Dale. In 1877 the company founded by Benjamin and Josiah became Stanton Ironworks Co. Sheepbridge Coal & Iron was founded in 1855, and in 1889 Markhams took over the already established firm of Olivers. In 1903 Bryan Donkin & Co relocated to Chesterfield, and three years later the Chesterfield Tube Co also opened for business.

BY CANAL, ROAD AND RAIL

❖❖

The Chesterfield Canal is one of the earliest in England, the survey having been undertaken by James Brindley in 1768. The original scheme to drive a cut to the navigable River Trent by way of Bawtry was altered following offers of financial assistance from business interests in Worksop and Retford - but only if the canal was diverted through their towns. Construction work began in the autumn of 1771 at Norwood, where Brindley and his assistant engineer John Varley were faced with the task of driving a 2893-yard tunnel, and building a unique flight of thirteen locks split into four groups. On Brindley's death in 1772, John Varley and Hugh Hanshall took over all responsibilities for construction and surveying. The tunnel was officially opened in May 1775, and when the canal opened in June 1777 it provided a boost to a flagging Derbyshire iron industry.

The principal traffic on the canal was coal, though considerable tonnages of stone, lime, timber, lead, iron and corn were also carried. In order to compete with the railways the canal company formed its own railway in 1845, but this soon merged as the Manchester, Sheffield & Lincolnshire Railway. Under railway control, the canal remained reasonably prosperous until the late 19th century, but traffic was declining. The real disaster came in October 1907 when the roof of Norwood tunnel collapsed. The railway company could not justify the expense of rebuilding it, and the section between it and Chesterfield was abandoned.

During the 18th century, improvements to the road network in north east Derbyshire were carried out. A number of the turnpikes, such as the Ashover-Chesterfield-Mansfield road, were promoted by the likes of the London Lead Co, and by the 1830s there were fifteen stage and mail coaches a day operating through Chesterfield. The Tally Ho operated the run from Newark to Manchester via Mansfield, Chesterfield, Bakewell, Buxton, and New Mills. The Telegraph ran on the Sheffield, Chesterfield, Alfreton, Belper, Derby and Ashbourne route; and the Royal Hope linked the town with Halifax, Huddersfield, Nottingham, Leicester and London.

The history of Derbyshire's main line railways began in the 1830s, and in September 1835 the North Midland issued its prospectus for an ambitious scheme for a £1,250,000 rail link between Leeds and Derby. George and Robert Stephenson were appointed joint engineers, George playing an active role in promoting the company whilst at the same time amassing considerable business interests along the route, including coal mines at Clay Cross and lime quarries at Ambergate. Also in 1835 the Midland Counties Railway proposed to extend their line from Pinxton to connect with the NMR at either Chesterfield or Clay

THE CHANGING FACE OF CHESTERFIELD

Since the 1980s Chesterfield has gained an international reputation for conservation, and any proposed redevelopment within the town's conservation area must be sympathetic to its surroundings. Chesterfield may have few

Cross. The original NMR station at Chesterfield was designed in the Jacobean style by Francis Thompson; it was the largest intermediate station between Derby and Leeds, although it had a relatively short life, being replaced in May 1870. The last major railway scheme of the 1890s in north-east Derbyshire was the grandly titled 'Lancashire, Derbyshire & East Coast Railway', which owing to lack of investment and opposition from existing lines never got anywhere near Lancashire or the East Coast.

The LD & ECR's principal feat of engineering is the 700ft long Chesterfield Viaduct, built to carry the line east over the River Hipper. Despite experiencing major problems with Bolsover Tunnel the line opened in May 1897, giving Chesterfield its third railway station.

outstanding buildings, but the half-timbered revival shops of Knifesmithgate, the medieval layout of the Shambles and the area around the Market Place with its Market Hall and associated open market all come together to give the town character.

It was not always so. In the 1950s, 60s and 70s councils and developers rushed headlong into ripping apart town centres and destroying communities. In Sheffield the Park Hall housing scheme was hailed by architects, planners and sociologists as being the most significant project in the country. They did not have to live there, however, and the gloss soon wore off. There were, and still are, problems with vandalism, and Park Hall soon became known to its inhabitants as San Quentin.

Chesterfield Borough Council was no different. It wanted to sweep away much of the town centre in the name of modernisation. It planned that the Market Place, Market Hall, New Square and the Shambles would be consigned to history, and in their place would rise a covered shopping centre spreading over five acres, topped off with a five-storey office block which would come with planning permission to go up to eleven storeys. What was to be left of the open market, and it was not going to be much, would be confined to a small area on the western end of the development.

At first opposition was slow in getting off the ground, but when people began to realise what was intended for their town centre they began to object - and the council found itself on the receiving end of the biggest public backlash in the town's history. By the time of a public inquiry in December 1967 no less than 204 objections had been lodged, and the inquiry sat for 32 days.

Despite objections, the council still planned to go ahead, obtaining permission to demolish any listed buildings (such as Nos. 41, 43 and 45 Low Pavement) that were in the way. Market traders weighed in with a 32,000 signature petition, but it was the Civic Society who hit the nail on the head. They stated that perfectly sound buildings were being needlessly pulled down and that the plan 'showed a lack of understanding of the aesthetic and symbolic value of buildings enduring in their original setting'.

Demolition work started. The Mansfield Vaults and the 'King and Miller' were among the casualties, and a demolition order on the listed Quaker Meeting House, Saltergate, was granted conditionally in May 1973 so that a multi-storey car park could be built. In February 1974 a fire at the already threatened Peacock Inn revealed that beneath the Victorian frontage lurked a much older tim-

ber-framed building. Even so, the Department of the Environment refused to list the building, and could not even be bothered to send inspectors to have a look at it.

By now both the Council and the Department of the Environment were getting bad press, especially in the Sheffield Star, the Sunday Times, the Observer and the Architect's Journal. On 1 April 1974, Chesterfield Heritage Society members served a writ on the Council claiming that the redevelopment 'would give rise to a loss or deficiency on the accounts of the defendants (the Council) which would be surchargeable under Section 228(1)(d) of the Local Government Act 1972'. There is nothing a councillor fears more than having to pay for

his or her mistakes through personal surcharge. A few days later, the Council were scuppered again when the developer pulled the plug, thanks to a combination of a downturn in the property market and Chancellor Anthony Barber announcing the introduction of a first lettings tax in the budget.

In 1977 there was a complete change of tack. It was suggested that the Market Hall be restored and reconstructed with a new western section, that original shop frontages be retained where practical, and that the Shambles be rehabilitated. The Market Hall was officially reopened in November 1981. The open market now operates three days a week drawing in shoppers from miles around, many turning the trip into a day out.

TRINITY CHURCH 1896 37803
Holy Trinity was built in 1838 at a cost of £3700 on land given for the purpose by William, sixth Duke of Devonshire. Restoration work in the 1880s included the strengthening of the roof timbers and building an organ loft. Further work on the organ was done in 1894.

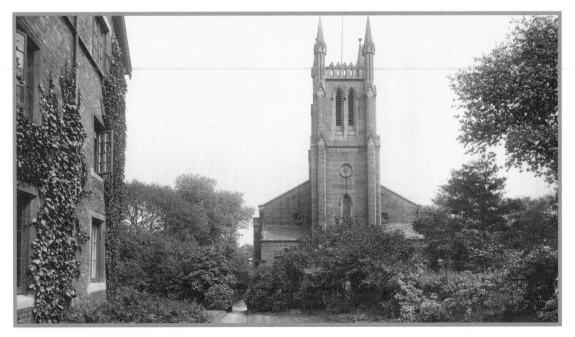

HOLY TRINITY CHURCH 1914 67567
The fine embattled western tower of Holy Trinity houses a clock and one bell. When Holy Trinity became an ecclesiastical parish in its own right in 1841 it included the West Park area, though this was taken away when the boundaries were adjusted in 1908.

HOLY TRINITY CHURCH AND THE STEPHENSON MEMORIAL 1914 67568

Railway engineer and businessman George Stephenson settled near Chesterfield at Tapton House and died there on 12 August 1848. He was interred at Holy Trinity beneath the altar and a stained-glass east window was also installed in his memory.

THE TOWN HALL C1955 C83023

The well kept gardens and fine central portico, supported on six columns, lend a touch of class to the imposing bulk of the Town Hall designed by Bradshaw, Gass & Hope and built between 1937 and 1938.

THE TOWN HALL AND ROSE HILL c1955 C83025
Once upon a time there was a house on the site of the Town Hall called Rosehill. In about 1830, when the tenant was a Mr James Ashwell, the bells used for calling servants to individual rooms developed the habit of ringing by themselves. Even the installation of a new bell system failed to stop these strange happenings, and they even rang after the wires had been cut. No explanation was ever found.

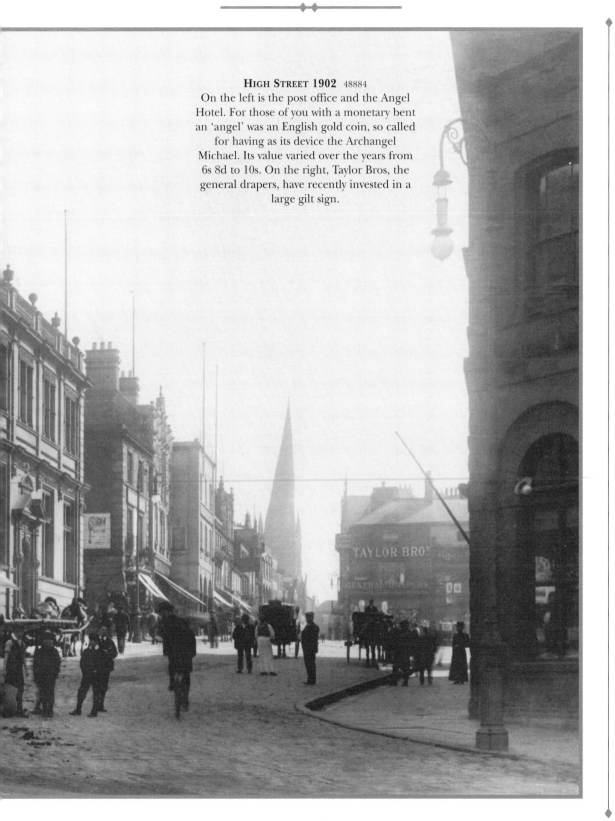

HIGH STREET 1902 48884
On the left is the post office and the Angel
Hotel. For those of you with a monetary bent
an 'angel' was an English gold coin, so called
for having as its device the Archangel
Michael. Its value varied over the years from
6s 8d to 10s. On the right, Taylor Bros, the
general drapers, have recently invested in a
large gilt sign.

HIGH STREET 1896 37801
On the left is Scales & Sons boot and shoe
establishment, formerly Scales and Salter. The
building next to Scales was demolished and the
site redeveloped for Spencer & Co. Across the
street next to Roper & Son is Taylor's drapery
store in its pre-gilt sign days.

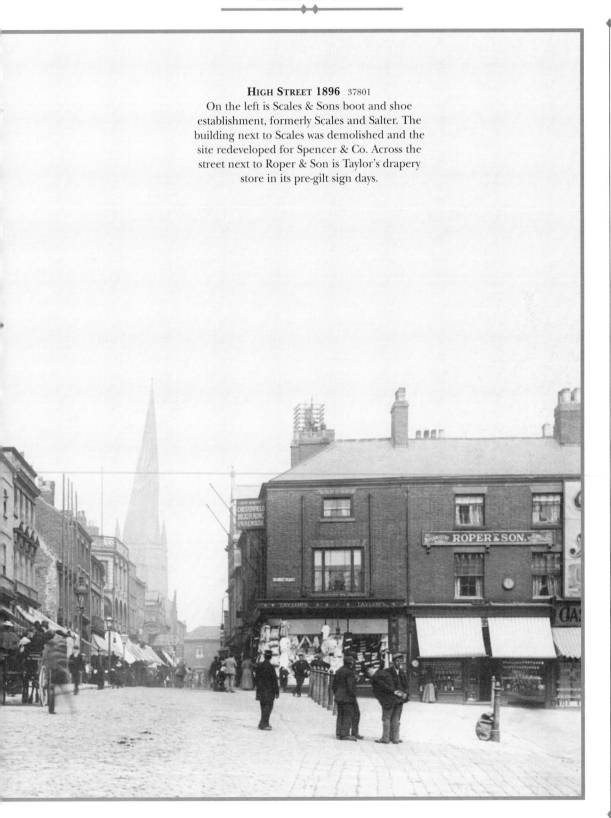

MARKET PLACE 1902 48882

The Market Hall was designed by Davies & Sons and completed in 1857 at a cost of around £8000. Included in the original structure was a corn exchange, library, mechanics' institute and a magistrates' court. The photograph gives us a good idea of the slope of the Market Place.

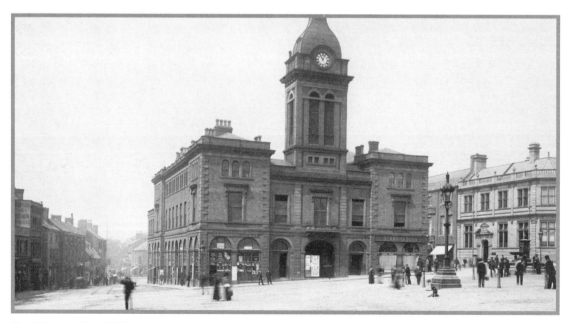

THE MARKET HALL 1896 37802

In the 1960s and 70s the Borough Council, aided and abetted by Derbyshire County Council, planned to demolish the Market Hall, New Square and The Shambles and sweep away the open market so that the area could be redeveloped. The plan was for a covered retail area embracing 80 shops topped off with an unsightly five-storey office block.

THE ROYAL OAK c1960 C83032

The Royal Oak is the town's oldest inn. Another old inn, the Peacock, was already scheduled for demolition when it caught fire in February 1974. Beneath the Victorian frontage was discovered a timber-framed building - the Peacock was far older than first thought. The fight against the wholesale demolition of the area lasted long enough for the Peacock to be saved and it is now the tourist information and heritage centre.

HIGH STREET c1960 C83038

The Midland Bank occupies the site of Scales' boot and shoe shop and Spencer & Co's grand frontage has fallen victim to an infestation of 'Magnet Ales' signs on behalf of the Wheat Sheaf.

HIGH STREET c1955 C83021

The post-war years saw the spread of high-street chains, and Chesterfield was no exception. In this picture we can see local branches of Timsons, Alexander, Burtons, and Boots. Just beyond Boots is Irongate, a part of the old town, with its medieval pattern of narrow lanes and alleyways. Threatened with demolition in the 1960s, the Shambles was saved and rehabilitated in the late 1970s.

THE PORTLAND HOTEL 1902 48898

In the tour guides of the period the Portland was 'well spoken of', with rooms from 3s 6d and lunch for 2s 6d. The Portland was considered to be equal to, if not better than, the Station Hotel: a rare accolade indeed when Britain's railway-owned hotels were amongst the best in the country.

KNIFESMITHGATE c1960 C83035

Though there is not a double yellow line in sight, parking on Knifesmithgate was restricted to just one side of the street, alternating daily. On the left is Tinley's shoe shop and just beyond that, though hidden from view, was the local branch of Redgates. On the right the King's Head has changed from Brampton Ales to Warwicks.

KNIFESMITHGATE c1955 C83014
There is still some debate as to whom, or what,
Knifesmithgate is named after. It is possible that
knife-making was carried on in the town; it is also
possible that the street was named after the
Knivesmith family.

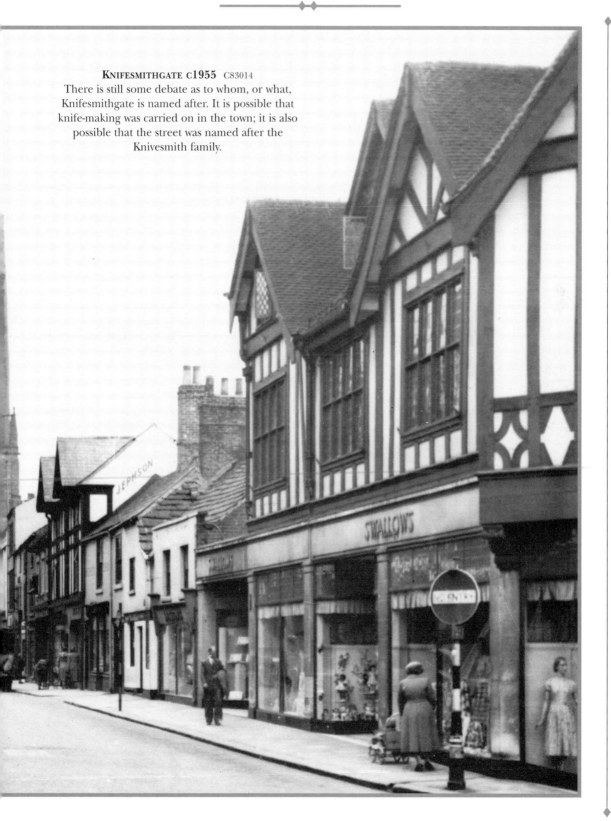

KNIFESMITHGATE C1960 C83031

On the face of it this picture is the same as the previous one. However, there have been a few changes in the details. The Victoria Cinema has become the Gaumont, and some modifications have been carried out to the front of the building. Timothy Whites down on Stephenson Place has a new frontage, and the billiards sign has been consigned to history.

KNIFESMITHGATE C1955 C83017
On the left is the Queen's Head Hotel; beyond that is the Chesterfield & District Co-operative Society. Directly ahead is the town branch of Barclays Bank.

STEPHENSON PLACE 1914 67563
This was named after George Stephenson the railway engineer, a canny Geordie who routed the North Midland Railway through Chesterfield. The large round building is William Deacon's Bank, the top floor of which is occupied by an architect's office and J. Marsden Chandler, surveyor and land agent.

STEPHENSON PLACE AND CAVENDISH STREET c1960 C83036
With the passage of time there are bound to be differences between this and the previous picture. Deacon's now occupy both floors of their building. There has been extensive redevelopment along Stephenson Place, and the tram lines are long gone.

STEPHENSON PLACE 1914 67565
A fine view of the parish church from Stephenson Place. The iron railings probably went for wartime salvage, and a part of the gardens disappeared to make way for car parking. The shop occupied by Stanley Bros later became an agency for Singer sewing machines.

THE CHURCH, SOUTH EAST VIEW 1896 37799
Despite looking as though it is about to topple over, the spire of St. Mary and All Saints is stable. The twist is a result of the heat of the sun on the lead plates, which in turn warped the green timber beneath them.

THE CHURCH 1902 48888

Tradition has it that the Devil visited Chesterfield one windy day and sat on the top of the spire so that he could have a good look at the place. To prevent himself from falling, Old Nick twisted his tail round the spire, but he was so shocked when he heard a local speak the truth that he flew off without unwinding his tail, causing the spire to twist.

THE CHURCH, SOUTH WEST VIEW 1896
St. Mary's was given to the Dean and Chapter of Lincoln in 1100, an event which probably took place shortly after its building. The oldest part dates from the 13th century. Both the tower and the south transept were added during the 14th century.

◆

THE CHURCH INTERIOR 1896
During the Napoleonic Wars, Chesterfield and Ashbourne accommodated French prisoners. Allowed out during the day, the prisoners at Chesterfield were summoned back to quarters by the ringing of a curfew bell from St Mary's. This bell was also known as the pancake bell, and used to be rung on Shrove Tuesday to call parishioners to their annual confession.

THE CHURCH, SOUTH WEST VIEW 1896 37796

THE CHURCH INTERIOR 1896 37800

THE PROCESSIONAL CROSS c1960 C83043
The processional cross once belonged to the Roman Catholic Chapel at Wingerworth Hall, seat of the Hunloke family. During the Napoleonic Wars, Sir Thomas Hunloke invited French prisoners to use his chapel. As Wingerworth was on the wrong side of a milestone marking the limits of the prisoners' freedom, Sir Charles simply had the stone moved.

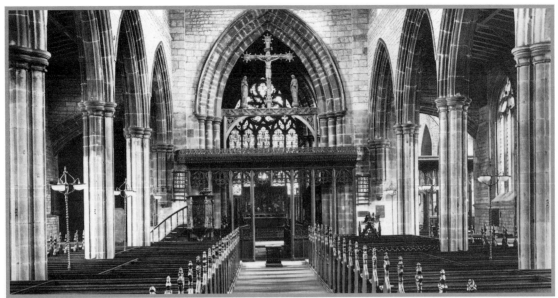

THE PARISH CHURCH 1919 69219

The Guild of St. Mary was founded in 1218 to protect privileges granted to Chesterfield by King John. It grew to become a powerful organisation within the town, and there was intense rivalry between wealthy local families for membership. One of the Guild's rules was: 'Each brother shall bequeath in his will, towards masses for the souls of his brethren, twelve pence out of every pound of his chattels; but he need not bequeath more than forty shillings in all'.

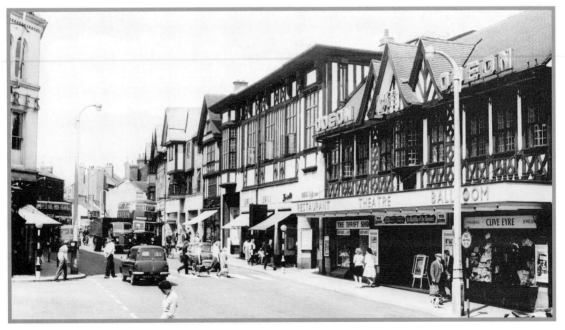

HOLYWELL STREET c1955 C83041

Holywell Street presents a rather pleasant picture of 20th-century half-timbered revival buildings, some of which would not appear out of place in Chester. The Peter Sellers and Robert Morley film 'Battle of the Sexes' is showing at the Odeon, but also of interest is the Thrift Shop, an early attempt at a discount store.

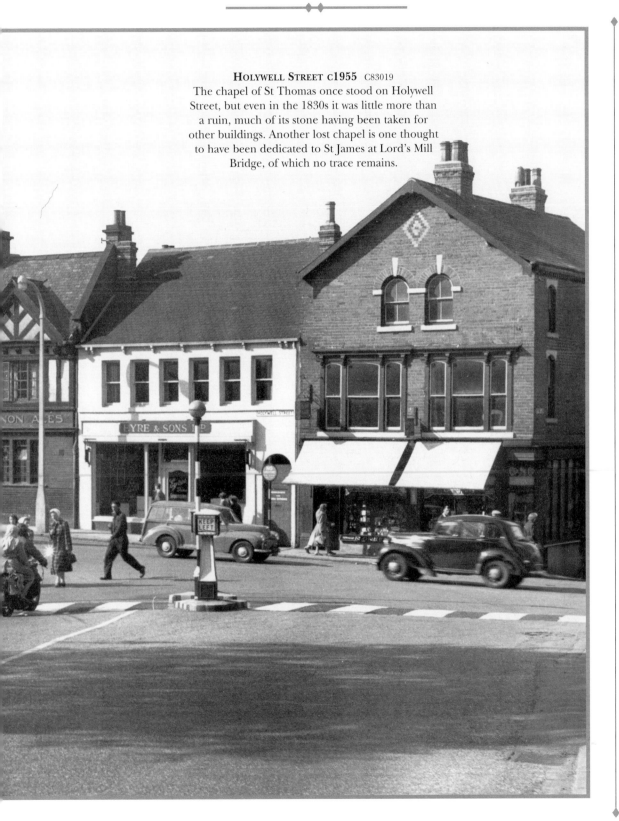

HOLYWELL STREET c1955 C83019
The chapel of St Thomas once stood on Holywell
Street, but even in the 1830s it was little more than
a ruin, much of its stone having been taken for
other buildings. Another lost chapel is one thought
to have been dedicated to St James at Lord's Mill
Bridge, of which no trace remains.

THE STEPHENSON MEMORIAL HALL 1902 48890

Situated at the head of Corporation Street, the Hall, designed in the plain Gothic style, cost around £13,000 to build. It housed the Chesterfield & Brampton Mechanic's Institute, the Chesterfield & Derbyshire Institute of Mining, Civil & Mechanical Engineers, and there was also a library, a public hall, some lecture rooms and a laboratory.

MIDLAND STATION 1896 37795A

The famous twisted spire of St Mary and All Saints leaves one in no doubt that this is Chesterfield. The Midland Railway station opened for traffic on 2 May 1870, replacing the somewhat smaller yet grander original station designed by North Midland Railway architect Francis Thompson.

THE RAILWAY 1896

Had the Lancashire, Derbyshire & East Coast Railway had its way, their main line would have run from Warrington to Sutton-on-Sea. They never got further west than Chesterfield where they had a station at West Bars near the Market Place, and extensive goods facilities. On this side of town the Midland operated a short goods branch to Brampton.

QUEEN'S PARK 1902

In 1902 there were over 27,000 people living and working in Chesterfield. Queen's Park provided them with an opportunity to escape from the grit and the grime. In the 1960s facilities were upgraded with the construction of a sports stadium and a running track.

THE RAILWAY 1896 37804

QUEEN'S PARK 1902 48893

QUEEN'S PARK 1902 48895
The antics of the Frith cameraman appear to
have drawn a small crowd of onlookers. It was
Frith policy that pictures intended for
publication as postcards be devoid of people,
or anything else that could give away the age
of the photograph. It was purely commercial;
Frith wanted their postcards to have a long
shelf life.

QUEEN'S PARK 1902 48894

The girl in the immediate foreground obviously liked having her picture taken, as she is also in Photograph No 48895. Of interest here are the prams; try getting one of these into the back of a Volvo estate car. The far pram is all the more interesting in that the design of the bodywork is ornate lattice-work.

QUEEN'S PARK LAKE 1914 67571

The boating lake did good business during the long hot summer of 1914. The 28th of June turned out to be hottest day of the year - hotter in more ways than one, as it was the day that the heir to the Austro-Hungarian Empire, Franz Ferdinand, was assassinated in Sarajevo, Bosnia.

QUEEN'S PARK 1902 48891
In August 1874, Derbyshire County Cricket Club played Lancashire at Chesterfield, using Chesterfield FC's facilities at Saltergate recreation ground. On becoming a first-class side in 1894, Derbyshire's home games were confined to the County Ground in Derby. With the opening of a cricket pavilion at Queen's Park, Derbyshire CCC returned to Chesterfield in July 1898 with a match against Surrey.

THE CRICKET GROUND, QUEEN'S PARK c1955 C83009
In the 1970s Derbyshire CCC temporarily ceased playing at Derby and the club gave serious consideration to a permanent move to Chesterfield. Proposals were drawn up for a new pavilion, indoor nets, and a banqueting suite at Queen's Park, but were turned down by Chesterfield Borough Council.

TAPTON HOUSE 1902 48900
Built in the 18th century, Tapton House is where railway engineer and businessman George Stephenson spent the last years of his life. George discovered top grade coking coal at Clay Cross, and the company he founded became known as the Clay Cross Co.

BRIMINGTON
The Parish Church c1965

Dedicated to St Michael, this particular church has seen much reconstruction. In 1796 the old tower was pulled down and a new one built, and in 1808 the main body of the church was demolished and rebuilt at a cost of £842. In 1847 the main body of the church was demolished yet again and rebuilt, while the tower was heightened.

◆

BRIMINGTON
High Street c1965

The High Street was home to the Chesterfield & District Co-operative Society No 2 branch, as well as Brimington Methodist Church. Wesleyan, Primitive and United Methodists each had their own place of worship.

BRIMINGTON, THE PARISH CHURCH c1965   B603006

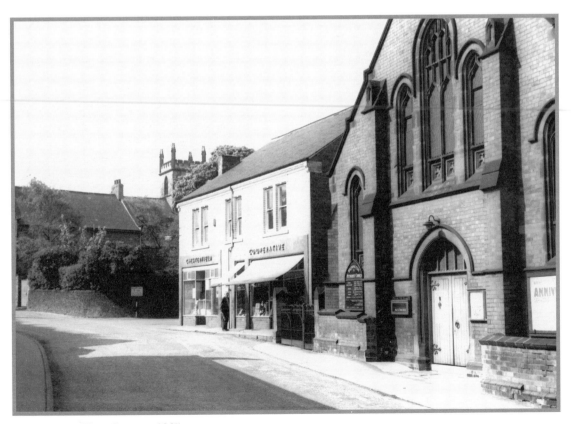

BRIMINGTON, HIGH STREET c1965   B603001

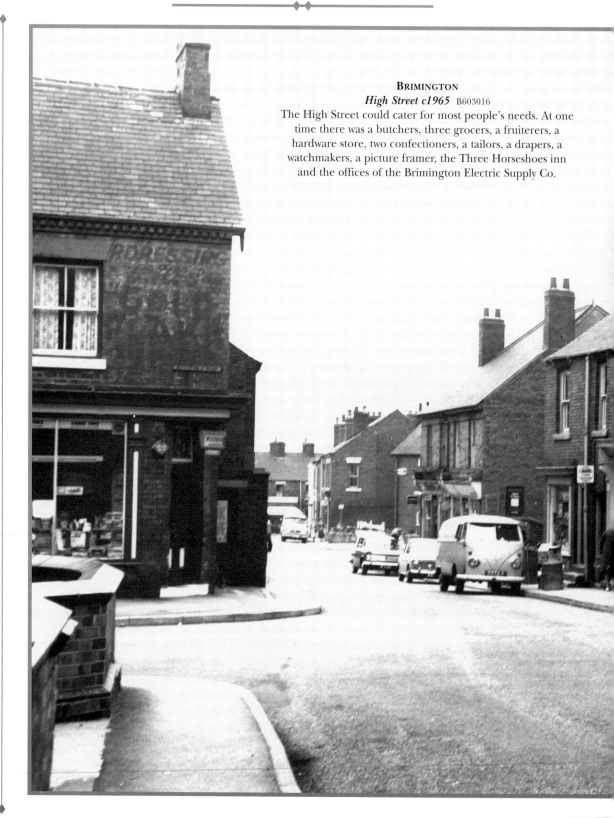

BRIMINGTON
High Street c1965 B603016
The High Street could cater for most people's needs. At one time there was a butchers, three grocers, a fruiterers, a hardware store, two confectioners, a tailors, a drapers, a watchmakers, a picture framer, the Three Horseshoes inn and the offices of the Brimington Electric Supply Co.

BRIMINGTON, MANOR ROAD c1965 B603014

The local garage is in on the Green Shield stamp craze; you were given so many stamps depending on the value of your purchase, which you then stuck in a booklet, each booklet holding a given number of stamps. When you had filled enough booklets you could trade them in for a gift. Shops soon started to try and out-do one another offering double, triple and even quadruple stamps.

BRIMINGTON, SECONDARY SCHOOL FOR BOYS c1965 B603012

A typical example of a late-fifties/ early-sixties school and college building; it seems monotonous and characterless. Early shopping precincts were the same, lacking in imagination and soon looking shabby.

DRONFIELD, CHESTERFIELD ROAD c1965 D177012
This photograph shows the old Midland Railway station. It closed to passenger traffic on 2 January 1967 and to goods traffic a few months later, though some private sidings continued in use until June 1969.

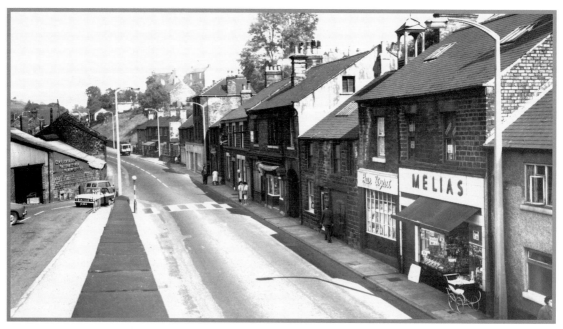

DRONFIELD, SHEFFIELD ROAD c1965 D177032

In the 19th century the town's industrial base boasted Samuel Lucas & Sons, ironfounders, spade, shovel and spindle manufacturers; George Ward & Co, who were spindle manufacturers for the worsted, cotton, flax and silk industries; scythe and sickle makers; a chemical works and a corn mill.

DRONFIELD, HIGH STREET c1965 D177041

Dronfield parish once consisted of the townships of Dronfield, Dore, Coal Aston, Holmesfield, Unstone, Little Barlow and Totley. Dronfield township's population was 2469 in 1851 and had risen to 5169 by 1881 owing to the expansion of the local iron industry.

DRONFIELD
St John's Church c1965

When the Domesday commissioners were doing their rounds in 1086, the most important royal manor in the area was at Unstone, which had its own church and a priest. No mention was made of a church at Dronfield.

◆

DRONFIELD
The War Memorial and White Swan Inn c1965

In the 1850s the locals' thirst could be quenched in the township's six inns and taverns; the Blue Posts, the Coach and Horses, the Green Dragon, the Greyhound Inn, the Horse and Jockey, the Red Lion and the White Swan. There were also four beerhouses run by Charles Fisher, Charles Frith, George Goodwin and Matthew Lowe.

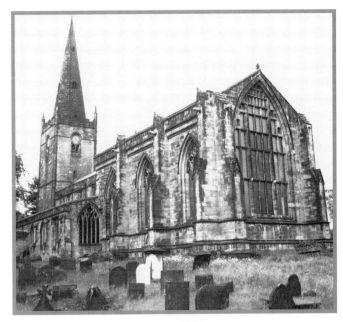

DRONFIELD, ST JOHN'S CHURCH c1965 D177039

DRONFIELD, THE WAR MEMORIAL AND WHITE SWAN INN c1965 D177048

OLD WHITTINGTON
The Revolution House 1902 48902
In 1688 this was the Cock and Pynot (magpie) Inn, and it was here that the fourth Earl of Devonshire and others met to arrange the overthrow of James II for his adherence to the Catholic Church, and to invite the Protestant William of Orange to become king.

ECKINGTON, CHESTERFIELD ROAD C1955 E226001

ECKINGTON
Chesterfield Road c1955

Eckington township is situated 6 miles north-east of Chesterfield and 7 miles south-east of Sheffield, and may be the place mentioned in the early 11th-century will of the Saxon earl Wulfric Spott.

◆

ECKINGTON
The Church and War Memorial c1955

Dedicated to St Peter & St Paul, the church here is first mentioned in 1310, though there was almost certainly a place of worship on the site in late Saxon times. The north aisle was added in 1746, the south aisle in 1764, and the main body of the building was restored in 1878. Further restoration works were carried out in 1907 (the chancel) and on the bells and tower in 1914.

ECKINGTON, THE CHURCH AND WAR MEMORIAL C1955 E226009

ECKINGTON, THE MEMORIAL AND WHITE HART INN c1955 E226020
A hundred years earlier in Eckington there were another five inns and taverns in the town: the Rose and Crown, the Duke of York, the Coach and Horses (whose landlord Jas Robinson was also a spring knife manufacturer), the Brown Bear and the Angel, from where William Lund also operated as a farrier.

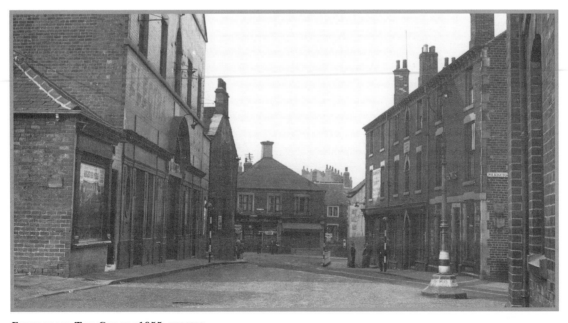

ECKINGTON, THE CROSS c1955 E226003
On the left is the Electra Cinema which occupied the ground floor of the defunct Market Hall. The Market Hall opened in 1879, the ground floor of 75ft x 66ft being sectioned off into a number of stalls. The upper floor provided Eckington with an assembly room complete with a stage, but this too was converted to another use - a billiards hall.

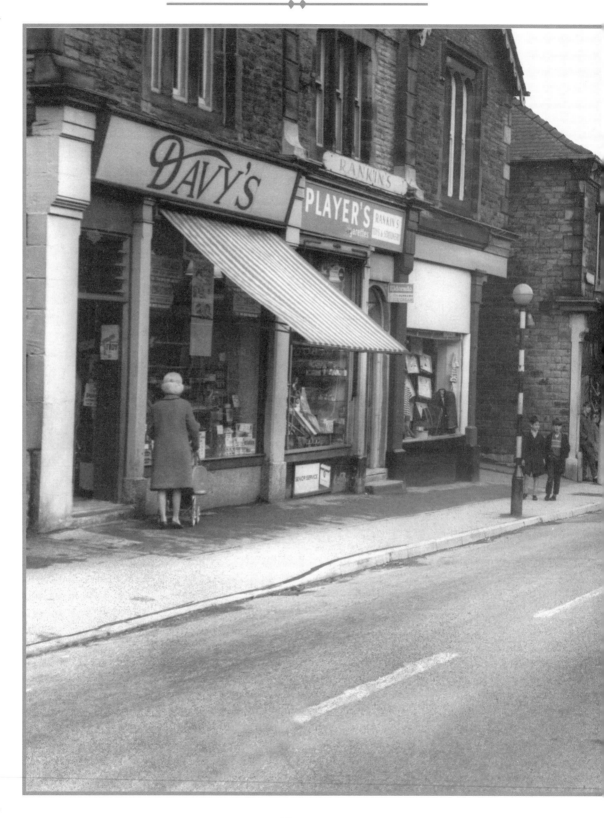

ECKINGTON
Market Street c1955 E226019
On the right, where Booth's fruit shop is situated, is the junction with Southgate which leads up to the Electra Cinema. In the 1930s Southgate also had a drapers shop run by Misses Lucy and Mary Fox (you might just be able to make out a Fox's sign in the previous photograph) and there was a temperance hotel managed by a
Mrs A Smith.

ECKINGTON, MARKET STREET c1955 E226027

Here we see the changing face of downtown Eckington, with new street lights and a modest attempt at redevelopment. Some of the Market Street businesses had been going for years. Among the long standing names are those of Joseph Stanley Courtnalls Ltd, Joseph Burton & Son (provision dealers), and Jas Woodhead (butcher).

ECKINGTON, HIGH STREET c1955 E226002

As well as having the parish church, Eckington was a Methodist stronghold. The first Wesleyan chapel opened in 1807, paid for by the Wells family in memory of George Wells. Eventually there were United Methodist and Primitive Methodist chapels, and a Salvation Army Hall.

RENISHAW HALL c1955 E226007

The original house was built by George Sitwell in 1625, much of which survives, though absorbed by the extensive rebuilding work carried out by Sitwell Sitwell in the late 18th century. He also spent thousands on decorating the house, most notably the dining room (1797), drawing room (1800) and the ballroom (1808).

BARLBOROUGH, THE HALL c1955 B803002

Barlborough was built by Francis Rodes, brother-in-law of the fourth Earl of Rutland and a member of a landed family who had been settled in Derbyshire for about two centuries. Rodes, who was appointed a Judge of the Common Pleas in 1585, also built halls at Hickleton and Great Houghton.

BARLBOROUGH, THE MAIN DRIVE c1955 B803006
'From Barlborough Hall the village is nearly half a mile; the road leads through a beautiful avenue of lime trees'. The main drive was a typical feature of country houses; the longer it was the more impressive, and they were laid out in such a way as to show the house off to its best advantage. Barlborough's was planted during the reign of William and Mary.

BARLBOROUGH, HIGH STREET c1955 B803025

Situated eight miles north-east of Chesterfield and eleven miles south-east of Sheffield, Barlborough's population in 1829 was around 630. By 1911 it had grown to 2080, many of the men and boys finding work in nearby collieries and iron works.

BARLBOROUGH, HIGH STREET c1955 B803023

Though Barlborough could be considered a pit village, there had always been a strong connection with the land. Crops included wheat, barley, oats, beans and turnips. During the Great War local farmers included Miss Lizzie Bradley, the Lancaster brothers, William Locke, Roger Arthur, George Atkin, Alexander Topham, William Passey and Henry Coupe.

BARLBOROUGH, PARK STREET c1955 B803024

During the 1950s the site of Barlborough Colliery was cleared, but in 1955 there was an attempt by the NCB to re-open Southgate Colliery in Clowne. Southgate had been abandoned in 1929 after severe flooding from the already defunct Oxcroft Colliery. The NCB wanted to use Southgate to connect with the High Hazel seams at Creswell, but after several years of expensive tunnelling the project was cancelled and the site cleared.

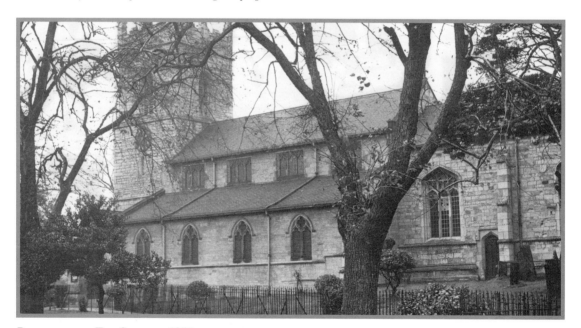

BARLBOROUGH, THE CHURCH c1955 B803016

The parish church of St James is thought to date back to the reign of either Henry II or Richard I, though it was heavily rebuilt about a hundred years after its original construction. In the 1890s rebuilding involved the demolition of the south side of the nave so that a south aisle could be added. Other work at this time included a complete refit of the interior and a new organ.

BARLBOROUGH
Church Street c1955

The pinnacled western tower of St James stands over the rooftops. In the chancel is a memorial to Sir Richard Pipe, Lord Mayor of London. For those who needed to wet their whistles after listening to a long sermon, the parish had six pubs; the Royal Oak, the Rose & Crown, the de Rodes Arms, the Blacksmith's Arms, the Crown & Anchor and the Dusty Miller.

◆

CLOWNE
The Technical College c1950

Clowne is situated about 9 miles north-east of Chesterfield. Many men found work at nearby pits, including Barlborough on the outskirts of the village. One of the reasons a college was established here was to provide educational support for the mining industry.

BARLBOROUGH, CHURCH STREET c1955 B803015

CLOWNE, THE TECHNICAL COLLEGE c1950 C403004

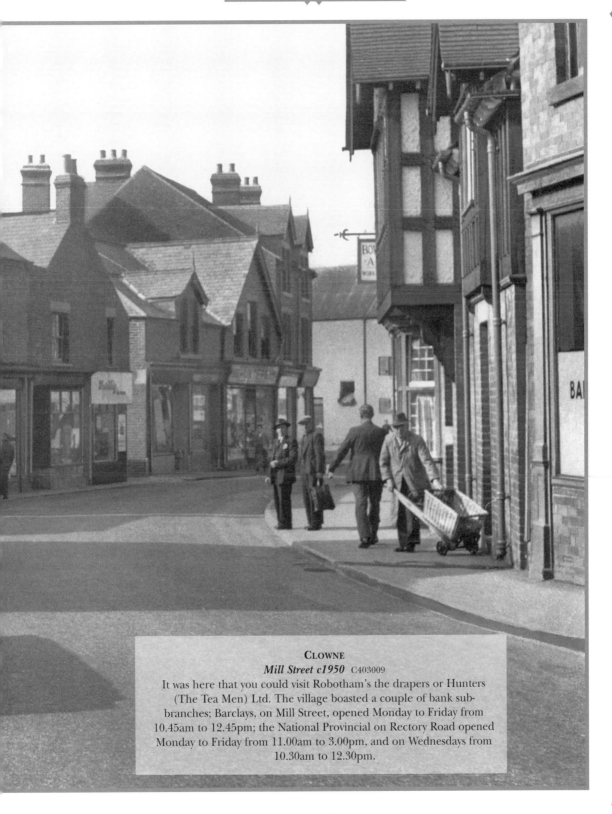

CLOWNE
Mill Street c1950 C403009
It was here that you could visit Robotham's the drapers or Hunters
(The Tea Men) Ltd. The village boasted a couple of bank sub-
branches; Barclays, on Mill Street, opened Monday to Friday from
10.45am to 12.45pm; the National Provincial on Rectory Road opened
Monday to Friday from 11.00am to 3.00pm, and on Wednesdays from
10.30am to 12.30pm.

CLOWNE, THE CROSS c1950 C403007
As well as the parish church and the village cross there are a couple of interesting memorials in the churchyard. One is a coped gravestone dated 1650, but considered to be much older; the other is a low headstone cross of which there are similar examples at Bakewell.

CLOWNE, THE CHURCH c1950 C403013

Dedicated to St John Baptist, the church was originally built in the Norman style, though much of this has been lost in subsequent rebuilding. In 1898 a new pulpit was installed and the churchyard extended by a further acre. Business appears to have been brisk, as the churchyard was extended again in 1925.

BOLSOVER, THE CASTLE c1955 B133027

There has been a fortress here since Norman times, though the present structure dates from 1613. It was built by Sir Charles Cavendish, who is said to have inherited his love of building from his mother, Bess of Hardwick. Though it looks like a fortress, Bolsover is in fact a magnificent stately home and of little military value.

BOLSOVER
The Castle 1902 48905

The ruins of the once luxurious state rooms at Bolsover Castle. It was probably in these rooms that the Duke of Newcastle lavished thousands of pounds on entertaining Charles I. One such three-day visit by the king in 1634 is said to have cost the Duke £15,000, a phenomenal amount of money in 17th-century England.

BOLSOVER
Market Place c1955 B133038
A village once famous for making spurs and buckles, Bolsover, like many towns and villages of north-east Derbyshire, expanded during the 19th century owing to coal mining. New Bolsover Model Village was built by the local colliery company for its workers and their families.

ASHOVER, EASTWOOD GRANGE c1955 A325023

ASHOVER
Eastwood Grange c1955
This is Eastwood Grange, but on the outskirts of Ashover are the remains of Eastwood Old Hall, built by Sir Thomas Reresby and blown up in 1646 by Parliamentarian troops commanded by that 'licenced ruffian' Sir John Gell.

BASLOW
Nether End c1955
Baslow, situated 8 miles west of Chesterfield and 12 miles south of Sheffield, was once a part of the parish of Bakewell, but became independent in July 1869, taking with it the hamlets of Bridge End, Nether End and Over End. These days Nether End is where most visitors to Baslow usually finish up; around the green there are a number of places to eat as well as several shops.

BASLOW, NETHER END c1955 B484004

BASLOW, THATCH END c1955 B484020

Thatched cottages are comparatively rare in this part of Derbyshire; to see Baslow's examples, you have to follow the signposted path for Chatsworth, which starts at the car park. Chatsworth is then reached by way of Queen Mary's Bower.

BASLOW, THE VILLAGE c1955 B484006

Frederick Barker was born at Baslow on 17 March 1808, and followed other members of his family by becoming a churchman. Frederick rose through the ranks to become Bishop of Sydney and Metropolitan of Australia (1854-1884). Following his death in San Remo he was brought back to Baslow, where he is interred.

BASLOW
The Bridge c1883 16576
Featured in this picture are the old mill (complete with waterwheel) and the medieval bridge over the Derwent, which has a toll booth at one end just big enough for one person to squeeze through. A second bridge was constructed in 1925 at a cost of £30,000, the land for the approach roads being given by the Duke of Devonshire.

BASLOW, THE GRAND HOTEL AND HYDROPATHIC ESTABLISHMENT c1884 16582

Guests were always welcome at hydropathic establishments, even when they were not taking water treatments. In 1906 pensions (daily rate for room and meals) at The Grand started at 10s 6d and were on a par with similar establishments at Buxton, where the rates varied between 9s and 16s.

CHATSWORTH HOUSE c1886 18644

Begun by William Cavendish, fourth Earl and later first Duke of Devonshire in 1687, the House was completed in 1706. The north wing was added between 1820-30. Royalties from the Ecton Copper Mine in the Manifold Valley enabled the House to be furnished on a lavish scale. Between 1760 and 1817 the profits from Ecton were in excess of £335,000 a year.

CHATSWORTH HOUSE C1886 18643
The annual running costs of a great house like Chatsworth are over £1 million a year, and apart from selling off the odd painting or other treasure such places have no alternative but to charge visitors an admission fee. In the days when this picture was taken the Duke was wealthy enough to allow visitors in free of charge.

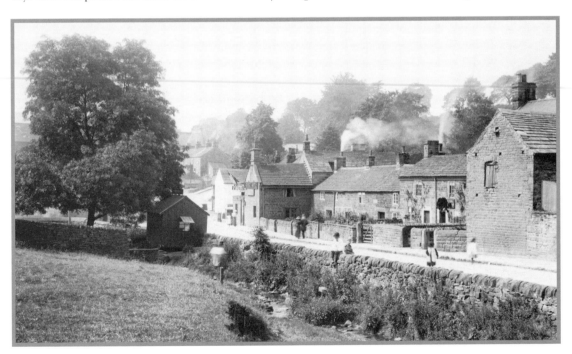

HATHERSAGE, THE VILLAGE 1902 48915
A small boy watches the antics of the Frith cameraman as he positions his camera for this picture of the main road to Sheffield. In the centre of the picture is the George Hotel as it looked before being completely rebuilt.

HATHERSAGE
The Village 1902 48914
The hillside village of Hathersage lies to the north-west of Chesterfield
and about 8 miles north of Bakewell, and is noted for some fine stone-
built houses, a church dating back to 1381, and its associations with Robin
Hood and Charlotte Bronte.

Index

The Surrounding Area

Frith Book Co Titles

www.francisfrith.co.uk

The Frith Book Company publishes over 100 new titles each year. A selection of those currently available are listed below. For latest catalogue please contact Frith Book Co.

Town Books 96pages, approx 100 photos. County and Themed Books 128 pages, approx 150 photos (unless specified). All titles hardback laminated case and jacket except those indicated pb (paperback)

Amersham, Chesham & Rickmansworth (pb)			Derby (pb)	1-85937-367-4	£9.99
	1-85937-340-2	£9.99	Derbyshire (pb)	1-85937-196-5	£9.99
Ancient Monuments & Stone Circles	1-85937-143-4	£17.99	Devon (pb)	1-85937-297-x	£9.99
Aylesbury (pb)	1-85937-227-9	£9.99	Dorset (pb)	1-85937-269-4	£9.99
Bakewell	1-85937-113-2	£12.99	Dorset Churches	1-85937-172-8	£17.99
Barnstaple (pb)	1-85937-300-3	£9.99	Dorset Coast (pb)	1-85937-299-6	£9.99
Bath (pb)	1-85937419-0	£9.99	Dorset Living Memories	1-85937-210-4	£14.99
Bedford (pb)	1-85937-205-8	£9.99	Down the Severn	1-85937-118-3	£14.99
Berkshire (pb)	1-85937-191-4	£9.99	Down the Thames (pb)	1-85937-278-3	£9.99
Berkshire Churches	1-85937-170-1	£17.99	Down the Trent	1-85937-311-9	£14.99
Blackpool (pb)	1-85937-382-8	£9.99	Dublin (pb)	1-85937-231-7	£9.99
Bognor Regis (pb)	1-85937-431-x	£9.99	East Anglia (pb)	1-85937-265-1	£9.99
Bournemouth	1-85937-067-5	£12.99	East London	1-85937-080-2	£14.99
Bradford (pb)	1-85937-204-x	£9.99	East Sussex	1-85937-130-2	£14.99
Brighton & Hove(pb)	1-85937-192-2	£8.99	Eastbourne	1-85937-061-6	£12.99
Bristol (pb)	1-85937-264-3	£9.99	Edinburgh (pb)	1-85937-193-0	£8.99
British Life A Century Ago (pb)	1-85937-213-9	£9.99	England in the 1880s	1-85937-331-3	£17.99
Buckinghamshire (pb)	1-85937-200-7	£9.99	English Castles (pb)	1-85937-434-4	£9.99
Camberley (pb)	1-85937-222-8	£9.99	English Country Houses	1-85937-161-2	£17.99
Cambridge (pb)	1-85937-422-0	£9.99	Essex (pb)	1-85937-270-8	£9.99
Cambridgeshire (pb)	1-85937-420-4	£9.99	Exeter	1-85937-126-4	£12.99
Canals & Waterways (pb)	1-85937-291-0	£9.99	Exmoor	1-85937-132-9	£14.99
Canterbury Cathedral (pb)	1-85937-179-5	£9.99	Falmouth	1-85937-066-7	£12.99
Cardiff (pb)	1-85937-093-4	£9.99	Folkestone (pb)	1-85937-124-8	£9.99
Carmarthenshire	1-85937-216-3	£14.99	Glasgow (pb)	1-85937-190-6	£9.99
Chelmsford (pb)	1-85937-310-0	£9.99	Gloucestershire	1-85937-102-7	£14.99
Cheltenham (pb)	1-85937-095-0	£9.99	Great Yarmouth (pb)	1-85937-426-3	£9.99
Cheshire (pb)	1-85937-271-6	£9.99	Greater Manchester (pb)	1-85937-266-x	£9.99
Chester	1-85937-090-x	£12.99	Guildford (pb)	1-85937-410-7	£9.99
Chesterfield	1-85937-378-x	£9.99	Hampshire (pb)	1-85937-279-1	£9.99
Chichester (pb)	1-85937-228-7	£9.99	Hampshire Churches (pb)	1-85937-207-4	£9.99
Colchester (pb)	1-85937-188-4	£8.99	Harrogate	1-85937-423-9	£9.99
Cornish Coast	1-85937-163-9	£14.99	Hastings & Bexhill (pb)	1-85937-131-0	£9.99
Cornwall (pb)	1-85937-229-5	£9.99	Heart of Lancashire (pb)	1-85937-197-3	£9.99
Cornwall Living Memories	1-85937-248-1	£14.99	Helston (pb)	1-85937-214-7	£9.99
Cotswolds (pb)	1-85937-230-9	£9.99	Hereford (pb)	1-85937-175-2	£9.99
Cotswolds Living Memories	1-85937-255-4	£14.99	Herefordshire	1-85937-174-4	£14.99
County Durham	1-85937-123-x	£14.99	Hertfordshire (pb)	1-85937-247-3	£9.99
Croydon Living Memories	1-85937-162-0	£9.99	Horsham (pb)	1-85937-432-8	£9.99
Cumbria	1-85937-101-9	£14.99	Humberside	1-85937-215-5	£14.99
Dartmoor	1-85937-145-0	£14.99	Hythe, Romney Marsh & Ashford	1-85937-256-2	£9.99

Available from your local bookshop or from the publisher

Frith Book Co Titles (continued)

Title	ISBN	Price	Title	ISBN	Price
Ipswich (pb)	1-85937-424-7	£9.99	St Ives (pb)	1-85937415-8	£9.99
Ireland (pb)	1-85937-181-7	£9.99	Scotland (pb)	1-85937-182-5	£9.99
Isle of Man (pb)	1-85937-268-6	£9.99	Scottish Castles (pb)	1-85937-323-2	£9.99
Isles of Scilly	1-85937-136-1	£14.99	Sevenoaks & Tunbridge	1-85937-057-8	£12.99
Isle of Wight (pb)	1-85937-429-8	£9.99	Sheffield, South Yorks (pb)	1-85937-267-8	£9.99
Isle of Wight Living Memories	1-85937-304-6	£14.99	Shrewsbury (pb)	1-85937-325-9	£9.99
Kent (pb)	1-85937-189-2	£9.99	Shropshire (pb)	1-85937-326-7	£9.99
Kent Living Memories	1-85937-125-6	£14.99	Somerset	1-85937-153-1	£14.99
Lake District (pb)	1-85937-275-9	£9.99	South Devon Coast	1-85937-107-8	£14.99
Lancaster, Morecambe & Heysham (pb)	1-85937-233-3	£9.99	South Devon Living Memories	1-85937-168-x	£14.99
Leeds (pb)	1-85937-202-3	£9.99	South Hams	1-85937-220-1	£14.99
Leicester	1-85937-073-x	£12.99	Southampton (pb)	1-85937-427-1	£9.99
Leicestershire (pb)	1-85937-185-x	£9.99	Southport (pb)	1-85937-425-5	£9.99
Lincolnshire (pb)	1-85937-433-6	£9.99	Staffordshire	1-85937-047-0	£12.99
Liverpool & Merseyside (pb)	1-85937-234-1	£9.99	Stratford upon Avon	1-85937-098-5	£12.99
London (pb)	1-85937-183-3	£9.99	Suffolk (pb)	1-85937-221-x	£9.99
Ludlow (pb)	1-85937-176-0	£9.99	Suffolk Coast	1-85937-259-7	£14.99
Luton (pb)	1-85937-235-x	£9.99	Surrey (pb)	1-85937-240-6	£9.99
Maidstone	1-85937-056-x	£14.99	Sussex (pb)	1-85937-184-1	£9.99
Manchester (pb)	1-85937-198-1	£9.99	Swansea (pb)	1-85937-167-1	£9.99
Middlesex	1-85937-158-2	£14.99	Tees Valley & Cleveland	1-85937-211-2	£14.99
New Forest	1-85937-128-0	£14.99	Thanet (pb)	1-85937-116-7	£9.99
Newark (pb)	1-85937-366-6	£9.99	Tiverton (pb)	1-85937-178-7	£9.99
Newport, Wales (pb)	1-85937-258-9	£9.99	Torbay	1-85937-063-2	£12.99
Newquay (pb)	1-85937-421-2	£9.99	Truro	1-85937-147-7	£12.99
Norfolk (pb)	1-85937-195-7	£9.99	Victorian and Edwardian Cornwall	1-85937-252-x	£14.99
Norfolk Living Memories	1-85937-217-1	£14.99	Victorian & Edwardian Devon	1-85937-253-8	£14.99
Northamptonshire	1-85937-150-7	£14.99	Victorian & Edwardian Kent	1-85937-149-3	£14.99
Northumberland Tyne & Wear (pb)	1-85937-281-3	£9.99	Vic & Ed Maritime Album	1-85937-144-2	£17.99
North Devon Coast	1-85937-146-9	£14.99	Victorian and Edwardian Sussex	1-85937-157-4	£14.99
North Devon Living Memories	1-85937-261-9	£14.99	Victorian & Edwardian Yorkshire	1-85937-154-x	£14.99
North London	1-85937-206-6	£14.99	Victorian Seaside	1-85937-159-0	£17.99
North Wales (pb)	1-85937-298-8	£9.99	Villages of Devon (pb)	1-85937-293-7	£9.99
North Yorkshire (pb)	1-85937-236-8	£9.99	Villages of Kent (pb)	1-85937-294-5	£9.99
Norwich (pb)	1-85937-194-9	£8.99	Villages of Sussex (pb)	1-85937-295-3	£9.99
Nottingham (pb)	1-85937-324-0	£9.99	Warwickshire (pb)	1-85937-203-1	£9.99
Nottinghamshire (pb)	1-85937-187-6	£9.99	Welsh Castles (pb)	1-85937-322-4	£9.99
Oxford (pb)	1-85937-411-5	£9.99	West Midlands (pb)	1-85937-289-9	£9.99
Oxfordshire (pb)	1-85937-430-1	£9.99	West Sussex	1-85937-148-5	£14.99
Peak District (pb)	1-85937-280-5	£9.99	West Yorkshire (pb)	1-85937-201-5	£9.99
Penzance	1-85937-069-1	£12.99	Weymouth (pb)	1-85937-209-0	£9.99
Peterborough (pb)	1-85937-219-8	£9.99	Wiltshire (pb)	1-85937-277-5	£9.99
Piers	1-85937-237-6	£17.99	Wiltshire Churches (pb)	1-85937-171-x	£9.99
Plymouth	1-85937-119-1	£12.99	Wiltshire Living Memories	1-85937-245-7	£14.99
Poole & Sandbanks (pb)	1-85937-251-1	£9.99	Winchester (pb)	1-85937-428-x	£9.99
Preston (pb)	1-85937-212-0	£9.99	Windmills & Watermills	1-85937-242-2	£17.99
Reading (pb)	1-85937-238-4	£9.99	Worcester (pb)	1-85937-165-5	£9.99
Romford (pb)	1-85937-319-4	£9.99	Worcestershire	1-85937-152-3	£14.99
Salisbury (pb)	1-85937-239-2	£9.99	York (pb)	1-85937-199-x	£9.99
Scarborough (pb)	1-85937-379-8	£9.99	Yorkshire (pb)	1-85937-186-8	£9.99
St Albans (pb)	1-85937-341-0	£9.99	Yorkshire Living Memories	1-85937-166-3	£14.99

See Frith books on the internet www.francisfrith.co.uk

FRITH PRODUCTS & SERVICES

Francis Frith would doubtless be pleased to know that the pioneering publishing venture he started in 1860 still continues today. A hundred and forty years later, The Francis Frith Collection continues in the same innovative tradition and is now one of the foremost publishers of vintage photographs in the world. Some of the current activities include:

Interior Decoration

Today Frith's photographs can be seen framed and as giant wall murals in thousands of pubs, restaurants, hotels, banks, retail stores and other public buildings throughout the country. In every case they enhance the unique local atmosphere of the places they depict and provide reminders of gentler days in an increasingly busy and frenetic world.

Product Promotions

Frith products are used by many major companies to promote the sales of their own products or to reinforce their own history and heritage. Frith promotions have been used by Hovis bread, Courage beers, Scots Porage Oats, Colman's mustard, Cadbury's foods, Mellow Birds coffee, Dunhill pipe tobacco, Guinness, and Bulmer's Cider.

Genealogy and Family History

As the interest in family history and roots grows world-wide, more and more people are turning to Frith's photographs of Great Britain for images of the towns, villages and streets where their ancestors lived; and, of course, photographs of the churches and chapels where their ancestors were christened, married and buried are an essential part of every genealogy tree and family album.

Frith Products

All Frith photographs are available Framed or just as Mounted Prints and Posters (size 23 x 16 inches). These may be ordered from the address below. From time to time other products - Address Books, Calendars, Table Mats, etc - are available.

The Internet

Already twenty thousand Frith photographs can be viewed and purchased on the internet through the Frith websites and a myriad of partner sites.

For more detailed information on Frith companies and products, look at these sites:

www.francisfrith.co.uk
www.francisfrith.com
(for North American visitors)

See the complete list of Frith Books at:

www.francisfrith.co.uk

This web site is regularly updated with the latest list of publications from the Frith Book Company. If you wish to buy books relating to another part of the country that your local bookshop does not stock, you may purchase on-line.

For further information, trade, or author enquiries please contact us at the address below:
The Francis Frith Collection, Frith's Barn, Teffont, Salisbury, Wiltshire, England SP3 5QP.
Tel: +44 (0)1722 716 376 Fax: +44 (0)1722 716 881   Email: sales@francisfrith.co.uk

See Frith books on the internet www.francisfrith.co.uk

TO RECEIVE YOUR **FREE** MOUNTED PRINT

Mounted Print
Overall size 14 x 11 inches

Cut out this Voucher and return it with your remittance for £1.95 to cover postage and handling, to UK addresses. For overseas addresses please include £4.00 post and handling. Choose any photograph included in this book. Your SEPIA print will be A4 in size, and mounted in a cream mount with burgundy rule line, overall size 14 x 11 inches.

Order additional Mounted Prints at HALF PRICE (only £7.49 each*)

If there are further pictures you would like to order, possibly as gifts for friends and family, purchase them at half price (no additional postage and handling required).

Have your Mounted Prints framed*

For an additional £14.95 per print you can have your chosen Mounted Print framed in an elegant polished wood and gilt moulding, overall size 16 x 13 inches (no additional postage and handling required).

---

* IMPORTANT!
These special prices are only available if ordered using the original voucher on this page (no copies permitted) and at the same time as your free Mounted Print, for delivery to the same address

---

Frith Collectors' Guild

From time to time we publish a magazine of news and stories about Frith photographs and further special offers of Frith products. If you would like 12 months FREE membership, please return this form.

Send completed forms to:
The Francis Frith Collection, Frith's Barn, Teffont, Salisbury, Wiltshire SP3 5QP

Voucher for **FREE** and Reduced Price Frith Prints

Picture no.	Page number	Qty	Mounted @ £7.49	Framed + £14.95	Total Cost
		1	**Free of charge***	£	£
			£7.49	£	£
			£7.49	£	£
			£7.49	£	£
			£7.49	£	£
			£7.49	£	£

Please allow 28 days for delivery	*** Post & handling**	**£1.95**
Book Title	**Total Order Cost**	**£**

Please do not photocopy this voucher. Only the original is valid, so please cut it out and return it to us.

I enclose a cheque / postal order for £ . . . .
made payable to 'The Francis Frith Collection'
OR please debit my Mastercard / Visa / Switch / Amex card
(credit cards please on all overseas orders)

Number . . . .

Issue No(Switch only) . . . . .Valid from (Amex/Switch) . . . .

Expires . . . .   Signature . . . .

Name Mr/Mrs/Ms . . . .

Address . . . .

. . . .

. . . . Postcode . . . .

Daytime Tel No . . . .   Valid to 31/12/02

The Francis Frith Collectors' Guild

Please enrol me as a member for 12 months free of charge.

Name Mr/Mrs/Ms . . . .

Address . . . .

. . . .

. . . .

. . . . Postcode . . . .

Would you like to find out more about Francis Frith?

We have recently recruited some entertaining speakers who are happy to visit local groups, clubs and societies to give an illustrated talk documenting Frith's travels and photographs. If you are a member of such a group and are interested in hosting a presentation, we would love to hear from you.

Our speakers bring with them a small selection of our local town and county books, together with sample prints. They are happy to take orders. A small proportion of the order value is donated to the group who have hosted the presentation. The talks are therefore an excellent way of fundraising for small groups and societies.

Can you help us with information about any of the Frith photographs in this book?

We are gradually compiling an historical record for each of the photographs in the Frith archive. It is always fascinating to find out the names of the people shown in the pictures, as well as insights into the shops, buildings and other features depicted.

If you recognize anyone in the photographs in this book, or if you have information not already included in the author's caption, do let us know. We would love to hear from you, and will try to publish it in future books or articles.

Our production team

Frith books are produced by a small dedicated team at offices in the converted Grade II listed 18th-century barn at Teffont near Salisbury, illustrated above. Most have worked with the Frith Collection for many years. All have in common one quality: they have a passion for the Frith Collection. The team is constantly expanding, but currently includes:

Jason Buck, John Buck, Douglas Burns, Heather Crisp, Isobel Hall, Rob Hames, Hazel Heaton, Peter Horne, James Kinnear, Tina Leary, Hannah Marsh, Eliza Sackett, Terence Sackett, Sandra Sanger, Shelley Tolcher, Susanna Walker, Clive Wathen and Jenny Wathen.